THE ENGLISH GENTLEMAN'S CHILD

THE ENGLISH GENTLEMAN'S CHILD

Douglas Sutherland

PREFACE BY
LORD ELPHINSTONE

DRAWINGS BY
TIMOTHY JAQUES

Penguin Books

Penguin Books Ltd. Harmondsworth, Middlesex, England
Penguin Books, 625 Madison Avenue, New York, New York 10022, U.S.A.
Penguin Books Australia Ltd. Ringwood, Victoria, Australia
Penguin Books Canada Ltd. 2801 John Street, Markham, Ontario, Canada L3R 1B4
Penguin Books (N.Z.) Ltd. 182-190 Wairau Road. Auckland 10, New Zealand

—

Published in Debrett's Peerage Ltd. 1979
Published in The Viking Press by arrangement with Debrett's Peerage Ltd, 1980
Published in Penguin Books, 1981

—

—

Manufactured in Canada by Webcom Limited

Acknowledgements

Robert Darley-Doran, whose interest in this subject inspired me to follow *The English Gentleman* and *The English Gentleman's Wife* with *The English Gentleman's Child*, will be for ever in my good books, as will Carol Illingworth, whose specialised knowledge of the feminine gender proved invaluable.

THIS BOOK IS FOR

my wife Diana and our siblings Carol, Fiona, James, Neil, Adam, Charles and Jo-Jo, together with any others whom I may have inadvertently overlooked.

Contents

Weather is no excuse for staying indoors

Preface

WHEN I was a child anything that went bang gave me an enormous amount of pleasure, the amount derived being in direct proportion to the size of the explosion. Now, in my twenty-seventh year this is still very much the case, which leads me to begin by asking the rhetorical question: When does an English Gentleman's Child graduate to being an English Gentleman?

In the light of my own experience, I would not dream of trying to answer that question. Certainly, as the author points out, the in-fighting in the nursery, into which the English Gentleman's Child is born, does a very great deal to equip him or her for later battles in the outside world. The hostilities practised in the nursery are not only Child versus Nannie. The fraternal and sororal struggles between the children themselves can involve campaigns of some magnitude, as well as having the added attraction of making Nannie very cross indeed. This is understandable when the outcome may involve little sister being removed by ambulance after her brother has been practising with his new set of bow and arrows, given by a well-meaning but unknowing aunt.

The fighting process is continued at school, when the English Gentleman's Child (if male) gains his first experience in the use of his fists. As I understand it, girls eschew this type of violent approach, indulging instead in a far more refined form of emotional torture designed to reduce the victim to tears at least a dozen times a day. I do not intend to make Gentlemen's children out to be ogres — indeed occasionally they can be charm and obedience itself. Nannies would doubtless put the emphasis on the word 'occasionally'.

I belong to the generation which has witnessed the virtual demise of the British Nannie. To what extent this decline will affect the English Gentleman's Child of the future is still open to doubt. I have a suspicion that perhaps the victory at Waterloo owes more to the nursery than to anybody's playing fields; whether hapless and less experienced mothers' helps will cope in the same way nannies did, I doubt. They are often too easy prey for engineered displays of wide-eyed affection and charm. This the long-serving nannie knows is a softening-up process after some particularly dreadful crime has been perpetrated. I was delivered out of the hands of the British Nannie at a fairly young age into the care of such less-prepared individuals. Remarkably, whenever we meet now they still seem pleased to see me. The last nannie who had the misfortune to look after me was packed off after it came to light that I was locked in a cupboard if and when I failed to perform the usual after breakfast function. In case anyone is interested this has not left me with any terrible hang-ups about that particular time of day.

My wife's nannie, on the other hand, is still in the best of health after presiding over the upbringing of not one, but three generations. Indeed at her eightieth birthday party recently, some rather ancient ciné films were produced showing her bathing her charges nigh on fifty years ago.

It is considered right that the English Gentleman's Child should spend a considerable time outside. Weather is invariably no excuse for staying indoors. It was easier to remain inside on the hottest day in July ('the poor little creature might get sunstroke') rather than on the coldest day in January ('children do not catch chills').

This leads to an early acquaintance with nature which,

aided and abetted by parental influence, rarely fails to interest the male of the species in bloodsports. Hours are spent designing Heath Robinson traps to catch the unwary sparrow; one of my most memorable achievements was to kill one of these unfortunates, high up an elderly elm tree, with a catapult.

Being of mixed Scottish and English parentage, I remain a little concerned about the title of this work. I have little doubt, however, that the attributes or otherwise of the Gentleman's Child are consistent whether he belongs to an English, Scottish, or Welsh Gentleman. That they might be bekilted or not, or pick up a different strain of vernacular while helping or hindering the gardening or gamekeeping staff, matters not a jot. A Gentleman's Child is a Gentleman's Child, and this book, apart from throwing some light on the various influences of heredity, education and environment (for those who are interested) shows that the Gentleman's Child still grows up in a curious world. This perhaps goes a long way towards explaining the habits, likes, and dislikes, which he carries with him, upon graduation, into the equally curious world of Gentlemen; a progression which Douglas Sutherland has entertainingly illustrated.

JAMES ELPHINSTONE

1

Post-Natal Impressions

I HAVE already remarked in an earlier study of upper class *mores* that whereas most English Gentlemen's Wives are ready (and in some cases, even eager) to have children, they hand them over as soon as they decently can to professional nannies to be brought up.

In many quite civilised countries this is considered to be a barbarous practice. It is particularly dismaying to American mothers who, mesmerised by the proselytising of folk heroes like Dr Spock, regard rearing their off-spring as a personal challenge, leading to 'the ultimate fulfilment'. In order to reassure themselves that they are on the right lines, this results in their pulling up their young by the roots at regular intervals to see how they are getting on. That this has resulted in the greatest gold rush for child psychiatrists since the discovery of the Klondyke is not regarded by American mamas as at all odd, or even relative.

Now, if I, with the benefit of hindsight, had to choose between the English and American child-rearing systems, I would plump unhesitatingly for the English, despite all its obvious imperfections.

The greatest gold rush for psychiatrists since the
discovery of the Klondyke

The reason for this certainty is hidden far back in my earliest childhood—in fact, when I was between two and three months old. (I have almost total recall of those early, formative months.)

I had already been handed over to my nannie (an Olympic swimming champion, as I remember) and was learning to trust her in such matters as not plunging me into overhot bath water and getting the temperature of my milk exactly right. Then one day my mother, seized, for some unaccountable reason, with a rush of maternal zeal, insisted on being allowed to change my nappies. Unfortunately, in securing the clean nappy, she also managed to spear an extremely sensitive part of my anatomy. The screams of outraged protest that followed happily convinced her that she did not have a way with children, whilst I myself became firmly of the opinion that the upbringing, certainly of young gentlemen, was far better left to the professionals.

In the chapters that follow I have tried to explain to those who have not experienced it how 'the system' works, and recommend the study to those of my readers who may be contemplating launching a child of their own into this cruel and changing world.

Lest, however, the description which follows of the way in which an English Gentleman's Child is normally reared be regarded as a gross exaggeration, I would like first to quote a passage on the upbringing of children of the French aristocracy in the eighteenth century from Duff Cooper's excellent biography of Talleyrand (Jonathan Cape). It may serve to show that the British system as we know it today is positively benign:

'The childhood of the French nobleman in the eighteenth century was not usually the period of his life upon which he looked back with either affection or regret. The doctrine that parents exist for the sake of their children was not then accepted, and the loving care and hourly attention bestowed upon the children of today would

[3]

have appeared ridiculous to sensible people. When Rousseau, the first man of sentiment, abandoned all his children, one after the other, to be brought up as unknown foundlings, his conduct was thought odd but not vile. The heir to the richest dukedom in France describes how his education was entrusted to one of his father's lackeys who happened to be able to read, how he was dressed in the prettiest clothes for going out but how at home he was left naked and hungry, and how this was the fate of all children of his age and class. The modern method reflects greater credit on the parents; but evidence is not yet sufficient to prove that it produces a superior type of individual.'

2

The Nursery

'THE nursery', suggesting as it does a clinically-clean room smelling of wax polish and disinfectant, is a misleading description of the place where Gentlemen's Children spend such a large part of their early years.

'Nursery quarters' would be more appropriate, for they frequently occupy a large part of a Gentleman's house, particularly if he is a fecund Gentleman. Even an only child rates a day and a night nursery and, of course, Nannie has to have her own quarters. Whereas there is only one day nursery, more and more rooms are called into service as night nurseries for as long as the zeal of the master and mistress lasts. In Victorian days Ladies and Gentlemen (as well as their social inferiors) continued to procreate at regular intervals well into middle age, but nowadays they are either less athletic or have the advantage of more advanced medical research.

Nor are the nursery quarters by any means antiseptic. Night nurseries tend to be comforting places to which their occupants can retire from the daily cut and thrust of battle. For many children their most happy recollections are of being tucked up with Teddy between sweet-smelling sheets, gazing drowsily at the flickering images thrown by the firelight on the ceiling with a comforting Price's night light burning dimly on the bedside table.

The day nursery, too, has its delights. The old rocking-horse long bereft of mane and tail, the toy cupboard into which all toys must be tidied away before supper, and the large toffee tin, kept safely out of reach but reassuringly available as a panacea for such minor disasters as grazed knees or as a reward for being a brave soldier and taking nasty medicine like a man.

Nursery training

Every nannie worth her salt regards the proper training of her charges as a sacred trust and, by and large, all nannies abide by the same rule of thumb methods which have been handed down from generation to generation.

(I do not here, of course, refer to those children's nurses — quite a different breed to nannies — who have been trained to the highest professional standards and come pre-packed in a special uniform which proclaims their distinction. A mother of my acquaintance who engaged one of these paragons told me that she was so overawed by her that it was only with difficulty that she restrained her instinct to salute her whenever they met.)

Nannie's approach to her task owes nothing to the modern theories or newly-discovered methods constantly being propagated (and often subsequently retracted) by the experts. Instead, she relies on a truth which has been recognised since Adam and Eve first invented children, which may be roughly translated as: 'If you don't get your foot on the little darlings' necks from the first moment you clap eyes on them and keep it there, you are not in with any chance at all.' This profound philosophy may be more succinctly, if less elegantly, expressed in our times as: 'Never give a sucker an even break.'

One of a nannie's first steps in the establishment of this dictatorship is in ensuring that her charges become house-trained at the earliest possible moment. Whilst it is a common problem all over the world, with the possible exception of places like Central Africa, where the dense bush makes it a matter of less importance, the method of the English nannie is in marked contrast to everyone else's.

The trouble with the vast majority of mothers is that they regard it as a battle of wits which results in the most absurd, not to say undignified, scenes. By no stretch of the imagination could one imagine any self-respecting nannie squatting on her hunkers beside some little mite, making encouraging grunting noises or cooing, through clenched teeth, such inanities as: 'Darling, *please* go potties for Mummie'; to which any sensible child's reaction would be to think: 'Why on earth doesn't she leave me alone and go and do it for herself.'

The standard nannie practice is quite different. She simply places her charge firmly on a suitable receptacle, looks him or her firmly in the eye, and says in a loud voice: 'Do your duty.' She then sets about other tasks, returning from time to time to see if her injunction has been obeyed. The result is that the child, left with nobody to do battle with, rapidly learns to concede defeat and reserve its energies for the next contest, which might offer a better chance of success.

Dumb insolence

There are several ways in which a very young child can put up a show of resistance to nursery government. One

Do your duty

of the most effective is by refusing to speak. Even the most upper-crust parents are not so lacking in parental affection as not to wait eagerly for the great day when their child makes its first intelligible communication. The sycophantic child will generally wait until a suitable occasion arises, such as when Nannie has brought it down to the drawing room to be shown off to an admiring audience, before making its maiden speech — something brief and to the point, like Ma-ma or Dad-dad.

Other children made of sterner stuff remain obdurately silent as months, or even years, pass. In extreme cases, distracted parents even go so far as to call in a speech therapist which, of course, is one up to the child.

One of the most successful examples of this ploy was a coup brought off by the young Lord Tennyson, who was in later life to demonstrate his command of the English language by becoming Poet Laureate. Young Alfred remained implacably silent until past his fourth birthday, thus throwing his devoted family into a state of despair. Then, one day, a careless nannie spilled some scalding water over his bare feet. Immediately she rushed from the room to find suitable salves. As she was about to apply them, the future Poet Laureate remarked coldly: 'You may desist in your efforts. The pain has now considerably abated.' A chess Grand Master could not have played the gambit with greater effect.

There must be many similar instances of heroic resistance which have, alas, gone unrecorded, but 'the system' would not have had the success it has down the years without having forged a foolproof formula which enables Nannie to deal with every possible contingency so that, in the end, there is no escape for the victim.

In the next chapter I shall reveal how 'the system' works.

3

The Nursery System

LIKE all well-planned operations, the essence of 'the system' is simplicity.

It relies entirely on there being an appropriate defensive stroke for every ball the child can bowl. As in this particular cricket match there is no onus on the batsman to score runs but simply to tire out the bowler, all that the Nannie is required to do is to play the ball straight back up the wicket and ensure that she is never caught out, stumped, or bowled. The cricketing analogy is not inappropriate because, of course, the game is played in the most gentlemanly way.

Here are some classic examples of attack and defence.

Attack: Nannie, what were you and Mummie whispering about in the corner?

Defence: Little pitchers have long ears (I never did discover quite what this meant).

Attack: Nannie, what does bum (or the current new rude word picked up in the stableyard) mean?

Eat up your lovely mince, Henry

Defence: That is a silly word. Clever people don't use a word like that.

Attack: Nannie, why do I have to eat my crusts?

Defence: Because they make your hair nice and curly.

Attack: But I don't like curly hair.

Defence: Little people don't say silly things like that.

And so on, ad infinitum.

Of course, Nannie sometimes has to abandon her entrenched position and take the offensive, as in:

Nannie: Eat up your lovely mince, Henry.

Henry: I don't like mince.

Nannie: If you don't eat up your mince you won't have any lovely pudding.

Henry: (impressed) What's for pudding, Nannie?

Nannie: (firmly, having just remembered that the pudding is more than usually beastly) It's 'wait and see' pudding, that's what.

Nannie's verbal dexterity is also used to advantage in recurring nursery situations, like when Henry hits Robert (little birds in their nests agree); Henry hits Mary (boys are stronger than girls and must be kind to their sisters); Henry makes a face at Nannie while her back is turned, forgetting that all nannies have eyes in the back of their heads. (Nannie, without turning round: If you make a face like that and the wind changes, it'll stay that way).

It is no coincidence that in later life Front Bench politicians who have served their time under nannies are far better at parrying awkward questions or getting out from under in a difficult situation than those who have not had the same advantageous start in life.

U-phemisms and non-U-phemisms

A great deal of nonsense has been written about so-called upper class speech, as if it were some sort of trap deliberately set by the socially assured to catch out the pretenders in their midst. Nancy Mitford's witty, but rather cruel, little joke which had the determinedly re-fined betraying themselves by calling mirrors looking-glasses, mantelpieces chimney pieces, and so on, has, one hopes, been finally consigned to the Great Joke Shop in the Sky, but some of the uncertainty for the socially ambitious lingers on.

Miss Mitford would have done a greater service if she had revealed the rules that successive generations of nannies have inculcated into their charges in their formative years, and which have remained with them for the rest of their lives.

It is, of course, far too big a subject to be discussed exhaustively in this modest volume. I will, therefore, content myself with laying down two rules which the Gentleman's Child quite unconsciously assimilates in the nursery and which singles him out in later life from the more liberally educated.

It is really very simple. All that is necessary is to recognise when it is permissible to call a spade a spade and when it should be called a shovel.

When a spade should be called a shovel

Perhaps the only clear-cut area in which the Gentleman's Child is subjected to the use of U-phemisms is sex. Oddly

Having been brought in his little black bag

enough this is practically the only area where the parents of less privileged children insist on explaining everything in graphic detail.

It is now considered 'the thing' for progressive parents and teachers at comprehensive schools to go to great pains to teach their children the technical words for all the working parts. Why this should be I am not quite sure. It may be, like so much else that is laid at its door, the influence of television. More simply it could be the thinness of the walls of the modern high-rise apartment blocks, or more simply still that Daddie can't be bothered to hide the latest copy of *Men Only*, which makes the necessity for parents to turn frankness on matters of sex into a virtue. Personally I am sufficiently old-fashioned as to have some sympathy for the child travelling with her mother on the top of a 19 bus, who was heard to ask in a world-weary voice: 'Mummie, I don't have to watch that boring sex film *again*, do I?' Nannies, of course, with their charges protected from the outside world, have no such problems.

All symptoms of emerging sexuality in their charges are firmly dealt with. Some nannies go on insisting, long after their children have left home and are about to have children of their own, that babies are found under gooseberry bushes. Others, knowing that a visit by the family doctor will not have gone unnoticed, favour the story of the new arrival having been brought in his little black bag.

Fortunately the sexual activities of the horses, dogs, and other animals with which a Gentleman's Children are normally surrounded, are considered fair game as topics for conversation. Otherwise many young scions of noble houses would be in for a considerable shock after they had been dragged to the altar of St Margaret's, Westminster.

Of course, there are some childish questions which are so blatantly sex-orientated as to drive even Nannie into a corner.

'Nannie, why don't goldfish get married?'

'That is a very silly question. Clever people don't ask questions like that.'

'Nannie, why does Henry always lift the seat when he goes to the lavatory?'

'That is a *very, very* silly question indeed. Clever people etc. . . .'

When to call a spade a spade

This applies to almost any subject where other people's children are taught to be devious.

One of the most bewildering things for the victim of a nursery and boarding school upbringing is the endless permutations of speech used by others to avoid the use of the word 'lavatory'. References to 'the littlest room', 'the hut', 'It', 'the powder room', 'the throne', 'the john', and countless other non-U-phemisms, are apt to give the monastically educated a feeling of inadequacy when first cast out into the world. A young man, asked by his hostess on arrival if he would like to wash his hands, cannot help noticing the sniggers when he replies: 'No, thank you. I washed them just before I came out.' This is the stuff that inferiority complexes are made of.

There are other even more sensitive areas where the English Gentleman's Child feels inadequate.

'Nannie, Nannie, why has that man got a black face?'

'Because he comes from Africa, dear, where the sun is very hot.'

(Supplementary question by intelligent child: 'Nannie, is that what Daddie means by calling a spade a spade?'

'*That* is a very sil . . .' etc., etc.)

It is misleading enough that Nannie should believe that all black men of whatever ethnic origin should come from Africa. How on earth can he possibly acclimatise to the fact that even to own a golliwog is considered to be an indictable offence by the Race Relations Board?

There must be a case for a Gentleman's Child spending some time in a rehabilitation centre before being released into civilian life.

What's in a name

Gentlemen, and in particular Gentlemen's Wives, pay great attention to the naming of their children. They show commendable concern in not saddling their off-spring with the sort of first names that would make them a laughing stock at school nor, like the car registration authorities, would they allow a combination of initials with embarrassing connotations. Few parents, for example, would saddle a male child with the name Evelyn and I am sure that none of the large Throckmorton family would choose Thomas Ian as forenames for any of their sons. Many parents, however, tend to perpetuate traditional family names handed down through the centuries. If these should ring strangely on the ear, like Pauncefoot or Fauntleroy, they remain a safely guarded secret behind the anonymity of an initial until the child is old enough or large enough to defend himself.

Unsafe names for girls are those derived from popular film stars, like Marilyn, Heidi, Tracy, Mae or Greta, flowers, like Hyacinth, Jonquil or Primrose, or jewels, such as Coral, Beryl or Topaz, pretty though they may be. Even Princess Margaret, who started out in life as

Nannie is so beastly to you behind your back

Margaret Rose, dropped the Rose after not very many years.

Safe names are any used by Royalty, like Elizabeth, Anne, Katherine and, of course, Margaret, which now has the additional cachet of being the forename of our first female Prime Minister.

Unsafe names for boys are virile American-derived ones like Earl, Duke, Wayne, Clint or Gary, or unvirile English ones like Cecil, Cedric, Eustace or Cyril.

Safe names for boys are any used by Royalty, such as Richard, Henry, Charles, William, and even Philip, or practically any of Christ's disciples, although the unwary should note that Judas has been out of fashion for close on twenty centuries.

Parental attitudes

If the impression has been given that a Gentleman's Children are almost totally ignored by their parents whilst they are in the nursery, it is one that must be corrected.

As I have observed in an earlier work (The English Gentleman's Wife), mothers make a point of visiting their children quite frequently and, unless something quite out of the ordinary prevents it, always see their children after they have been washed, powdered, and tucked up in bed for the night.

Because Mummie remains remote from their daily battles, she is held in the eyes of her children in much the same awe as a High Court Judge. Indeed, it is a role that she is sometimes required to fulfil. The struggle for power in the nursery sometimes involves some fairly vicious in-fighting. A nannie, driven in desperation to complain about the rebelliousness of her charges, may find herself outmanoeuvred by cunning children. When the caring mum takes them aside and asks them why they are so naughty, they are apt to open their big blue eyes and say something like: 'Oh, you see, Mummie, Nannie is so beastly about you behind your back we feel we have to stick up for you.' The mother, forced to decide between the possible hypocrisy of Nannie or the mendacity of her children, usually finds that blood is thicker than water and the chauffeur is summoned the next day to drive Nannie and her cabin trunk to the station.

As in the game of Cowboys and Indians, so beloved by children all over the world, another Indian has bitten the dust.

4

An Introduction to Education

GENTLEMEN, by and large, send their children to
boarding schools. Their opting to pay money for
something that could be had free results in a great
number of other people, who spend much of their time
researching ways of avoiding paying for anything they
can make somebody else pay for, gnashing their teeth and
frothing at the mouth.

Gentlemen, who are usually simple-minded folk, find
this difficult to understand. Reviled on all sides for
involving themselves in blood sports on the grounds that
they are cruel, they see little difference in doing what they
consider to be their duty in keeping down the foxes and
their duty in bringing up their children.

There are few people who would argue that the fox-
hunting Gentleman is doing the fox any favours. He is
therefore understandably surprised, having condemned
his own flesh and blood to something like ten years' penal
servitude, that he should be so bitterly attacked for giving
them an unfair advantage over the majority of children
who have more humane fathers.

That there are many Gentlemen's Children who agree

with this great majority is not to be disputed. The view of the average victim of the boarding school system was put in a nutshell by one little ink-stained beast serving his time at that prestigious establishment known to the irreverent as Slough Grammar School, but to the more conventional as Eton College.

Singled out by a well-meaning visiting dignitary for a patronising pat on the head and the stock question:

'And what, my boy, is your ambition?'
The ungrateful brat replied:
'To be an Old Etonian, Sir.'

A rose by any other name

Contrary to public opinion, public schools are not hotbeds of snobbery. In fact, those who have survived the experience never thereafter refer to their *alma mater* as a public school. To say, for example, 'When I was at public school' is the sort of statement deliberately designed to impress the impressionable. After all, others do not inflict their audience with remarks like 'When I was at comprehensive' or 'During my spell at borstal' unless they have some kind of chip on their shoulder about it.

The only exception is that, in the interests of chronological exactitude, people do say: 'When I was at my prep school.' All subsequent education is simply referred to as 'school'.

(It should however be noted here, particularly by American readers, that by no stretch of the imagination could the term 'public school' denote that it is in any way public, being so private that in some cases even the children of very rich persons indeed may find it hard to gain admittance.)

Wearing their old school tie in bed

Private school, boarding school, *et al*, are equally unacceptable for the same reason.

It is, however, perfectly permissible for Gentlemen's wives or daughters to refer to their convent boarding school as 'the Convent'.

The only exceptions to this becoming modesty are Old Etonians. They get round the difficulty by wearing their old school tie in bed, having their secretaries circle the fourth of June (Founder's Day to you) in their diaries early in January, and rabbitting on about Wet Bobs and Dry Bobs, being members of Pop, calling terms 'halfs', when patently they are 'thirds', insisting on calling their housemaster 'm'tutor', and much gobbledy-gook besides.

Harrovians get something of their own back by referring to their traditional rivals as 'the other place'.

I, being an alumnus of quite another place altogether, must now beg forgiveness for bitching — the stock in trade of those who are put in the position of trying to appear modest about what they secretly feel makes them inately superior.

I will now try to describe what they all feel they have to be superior about, without actually having to spell it out.

5

The Happiest Days of Your Life

Preparatory schools

WERE Gentlemen's Children to be plunged straight into public school after being severed from Nannie's apron strings it is doubtful if many would survive the shock.

It is for this reason that the preparatory school exists; there the children can be prepared for the rigours of the future. Although many prep schools can trace their history over hundreds of years, they have recently acquired a new-found popularity because the Queen, her sister and her royal cousins have all sent their children to such establishments.

Prep school, compared to what is to come later, is not a bed of roses, but they do permit certain concessions. For example, both boys and girls are usually allowed to bring with them their favourite cuddly toy. This is supposed to make separation from their families more bearable as they can hug it tightly as they cry themselves to sleep each night.

For the most part, however, prep school marks the beginning of the hardening-up process which will enable them to survive the next stage in their education. A cold bath every morning gives a properly stimulating start to the day. This entails complete immersion rather like the baptismal rights of certain religious sects.

The day itself is punctuated by the ringing of a very loud bell denoting the start and finish of a lesson, and practically everything else from morning prayers to lights out.

Most important of all, it is at prep school that the first seeds are sown of what boarding schools are all about — to inculcate in their charges a competitive sense. Where nowadays the tendency is to bring everyone down to the speed of the slowest and to discourage such things as exams on the grounds that they may induce a sense of inferiority in the less academically bright, the boarding school sets out to do just the opposite.

Class lists are pinned up on the notice board at frequent intervals and studied with all the earnestness that racing addicts devote to the form book. Every afternoon, whatever the weather, is devoted to competitive games. If the weather is so atrocious that nobody can stand up on the rugger pitch, the whole school is sent on a ten-mile cross-country run.

There are cups awarded for every conceivable activity, and sharp cuts across the bottom with a cane for anyone considered not to be trying hard enough.

I can remember one contemporary of mine being quite unjustly accused of some crime. He in fact managed to convince the headmaster of his innocence only to be told: 'You are a thoroughly scruffy boy anyway, so six of the best won't do you any harm. Bend over.'

On the whole the canings are easier to bear than the beastly cups. It is the appalling conceit of the more vulgar parents to present cups bearing their names, hoping to

Allowed to bring with them their favourite cuddly toy

create thereby memorials to their generosity. No school that I have ever heard of has ever been known to refuse a cup, but the name of the donor is reviled ever after by succeeding generations of schoolboys.

The most dreadful example of cup-giving that I can recall at my old prep school was one called the Hoosen Vase, which was presented annually to 'the most improved boy in the school'. The winner of the title was decided by a democratic vote of his fellows, all of whom were required to write an essay giving the reasons for their choice. Apart from the agonies of composition this involved, it was also the occasion for much crude lobbying for support, typified by such remarks as: 'You jolly well vote for me, you filthy little rotter, or I'll punch your head in.' It was no coincidence that this particular cup was always won by the largest boy in the school.

Skiving

The young schoolboy soon learns that it is almost impossible to be ill. Even if he wakes with all the symptoms to Blackwater fever and manages to crawl on his hands and knees to collapse unconscious on the floor of matron's room, he will get scant sympathy. Perhaps five minutes sitting quietly in a chair, a dessertspoonful of Syrup of Figs and: 'Run along now, young Jones, or you'll be late for your Latin class.'

This attitude to illness is something that becomes so ingrained in Gentlemen that it lasts them all their lives, and, indeed, Gentlemen become ill much less frequently than lesser mortals.

I remember, not very long ago, being told by a very gentlemanly Gentleman that a friend of mine had died unexpectedly. Naturally I asked what he had died of.

Five minutes sitting quietly in a chair

'I really don't know', replied my friend, adding, 'But I don't imagine it can have been anything very serious.'

Protocol

It is vital to the first termer that he should learn his place as quickly as possible. Quite obviously he must treat all masters with the utmost respect and the headmaster as a latter-day Jehovah, but his relationship with other boys is a rather more intricate matter. As a first termer he is the lowest of the low, and can really only communicate on terms of equality with those in the same position. At the same time equality does not mean being on terms of such intimacy as using first names. All schoolboys call each other by their surnames unless they happen to have known each other from pre-school days. Even then first names should only be used in private.

It is not done for senior boys to be seen hobnobbing with their juniors.

In order to avoid confusion over boys with the same surname, they are addressed in order of age seniority as Smith Major, Minor, Tertius, Quartus, and so on. When Smith Major leaves all the other Smiths are numerically promoted which makes it all just that little bit more difficult.

One of the ways round this formalised inter-relationship is the use of nicknames, and these too present certain peculiar anomalies.

Under no circumstances would a boy be saddled with the sort of nickname used by Other Ranks in the Forces. No Miller would be called Dusty, no White Chalky, no Clark Nobby, no Bird Dicky. Nor would any boy be nick-named Mick, Jock, or Paddy because of his nationality.

By the same token a very tall boy would not be called Lofty nor a very small one Titch.

Nicknames are usually of a derisory nature so, conversely, a tall boy might be called Titch and a small one Lofty. This is perhaps in line with the general rule that nicknames still fulfil their original purpose of concealing the owner's identity. On the other hand a very dark-skinned boy would almost certainly be known as Nigger, and a very fat one Guts. P.G. Wodehouse's books provide a wealth of fascinating nicknames; Oofie, Catsmeat, Bingo, Stilton, and so on. Other nicknames are less obvious and tend to stick for the rest of the boy's life. Nobody now knows, for example, why the present Lord Arran is universally known as Boofy.

Until I got used to it, I personally resented being called Blear Minor simply because my elder brother was known as Blear Major on account of the fact that he registered his disapproval of school by wearing a constant look of glazed indifference.

Prep school, in short, is a microcosm of the public school, which is the next inevitable step in the education of the Gentleman's Children. But before getting on to that, let's have a look at how they are developing in the holidays.

6

Oh, To Be Beside the Seaside

GENTLEMEN'S Children do not think of holidays in quite the same way as other people's children.

No child would be likely to say to another child at school: 'Where are you going for your hols?', simply because the inevitable answer would be 'Home'.

This is because Gentlemen do not spend agonising weeks shortly after Christmas poring over glossy brochures and arguing with their wives whether it is going to be Benidorm or Majorca this summer. By and large Gentlemen and their families do not 'go on holiday' in the sense of packing the sun tan oil and the dark glasses, counting on the charter company to have booked them in at an hotel with indoor sanitation that actually works.

If Gentlemen go away at all, it is to do something like shooting grouse or catching salmon, or paying the annual visit to his wife's parents. None of these activities, and particularly the last, is regarded as taking a holiday. They are traditional duties to be performed each in its proper season.

On the other hand, the word 'holiday' has magical connotations for the Gentleman's Children. As the end of term starts to loom nearer most of them make calendars, crossing off the days as they crawl past, much in the same way as prisoners mark the days off on the walls of their cells as their time for parole approaches. During the final week they start chanting ludicrous verses which vary from one establishment to another. Even now I can remember some of the time-honoured lines from my school liturgy.

> No more Latin, no more French,
> No more sitting on my bench,
> No more tadpoles in my bath,
> Trying hard to make me laugh.
> No more beetles in my tea
> Making googley eyes at me . . .

The day before final departure excitement would reach fever pitch, occupied as the time was with packing the school trunk and reserving the by now long-empty tuck box for such last-minute items as pyjamas, dressing gown, and sponge bag.

And then the Great Day itself when, sick with excitement, we were piled into the school bus and driven to the station, where the train was *always* standing waiting in the station, puffing as if as impatient as its young passengers to be off.

Could do better

Of course it is one of the cruel truths of life that anticipation is seldom related to reality.

First the rapturous reunion with Mummie and Daddie — a big hug from Mummie and a warm handshake from Daddie (fathers never kiss their sons, only their daughters and then rather perfunctorily), and then the first small cloud appears on the horizon.

Father: 'And where did you come in class?'

No more beetles in my tea

A simple enough question, no doubt kindly meant, but a sharp reminder that in a couple of weeks the dreaded easily-recognisable envelope (which will reveal all) will be brought in on the butler's tray at breakfast — the school report.

Remembering the merciless precision of school reports in my day, recording as they did the exact marks obtained in each subject, annotated by the appropriate master with comments which varied from the mildly approving to downright scathing, I was appalled to see a modern comprehensive school report recently. The only indication given to the anxious parents of their offspring's academic progress was by putting ticks in boxes to indicate whether they were above average, average, or below standard. On the other hand I could not help envying the child the smokescreen which so effectively concealed its more glaring deficiencies.

Most terrifying of all in the old-style school report was the headmaster's final summing up, which gave the more sadistic ones an opportunity of displaying their wit. I remember a particularly devastating footnote on one report (fortunately not mine but my brother's) which read: 'An extremely popular boy with everyone — except those who have the misfortune of having to try to teach him anything.'

Although holiday time is a happy one for the child by comparison with the monasticism of school life, it does not in any way represent a let-up on the necessity of being competitive.

Although Nannie will still be sitting in her rocking chair, placidly sewing on buttons, darning socks, and insisting on administering regular doses of cascara evacuant, she will have retired from the front line of battle and, however beastly she may have been in her hey-day, she becomes increasingly the object of nostalgic affection.

Her erstwhile charges will now have sterner matters to contend with.

The most serious misdemeanour of which a child can be guilty in the eyes of his parents is to sit around doing nothing. Doing nothing includes such things as collapsing exhausted in an arm chair after a particularly strenuous game, or, even worse, curling up with a good book.

'Oh do take your nose out of that beastly book. You will *ruin* your eyes. Why don't you go out and play in the nice warm rain?'

Games are constantly being organised. Tennis tournaments are arranged with beastly cousins and neighbouring children, French cricket, rounders, croquet, prisoner's base, treasure hunts, and so on, which would be impossible for lucky children in small houses with neat gardens. Almost all Gentlemen's Children are brought up in country houses surrounded by simply acres and acres of jungle and mossy lawns.

Even nightfall does not bring release from the necessity to compete. With enormous high-ceilinged rooms downstairs and a labyrinth of corridors, bedrooms, and cupboards, everyone—grown-ups and children alike—are pressed into taking part in games like murder, sardines, musical chairs, and charades.

Growing up

It is only when his children are on the verge of becoming teenagers that Gentlemen begin to acknowledge that there is a difference between their sons and daughters. This awareness manifests itself mainly in encouraging the girls to become competitive in pony clubs and boys to

Why don't you go and play in the nice warm rain?

take the first steps towards becoming proficient at blood sports.

No traditionally-minded parent would think of saying at breakfast: 'It looks like being a lovely day. Let's all go to the seaside.' A much more likely remark would be: 'It looks like being a lovely day. Let's go out and kill something.'

My father, who was basically a kindly man, could become a tyrant when out shooting—rather like those mild-mannered sailing chaps who become Captain Blighs when they get you on their boat.

One instance of my father's intolerance has remained with me with great clarity down the years. It was a bitterly cold New Year's Day, and for the first time I was considered old enough to join the grown-ups on the shoot traditionally fixed on that day to clear the cobwebs resulting from seeing in the New Year.

Equipped with a .410 and proudly carrying a game bag, I started out in fine fettle. Unfortunately in my enthusiasm I volunteered to carry the hares which most people avoid like the plague. Six large hares in a game bag are not much fun, even for a grown man. Finding myself thus weighed down I was suddenly faced with an obstacle of Beecher's Brook proportions—a four-foot wide muddy stream in spate with a bank on the far side topped by a thorn hedge and a barbed wire fence. I took a deep breath and a wild leap, missed my grab at the fence and fell back up to my waist into the icy water.

At this point my father, glancing down the line, caught sight of my plight and yelled: 'Get out of that water, boy. You are wetting my game!'

Back to the treadmill

The time when a child is conscious of how enjoyable his holidays have been is when he realises with a sinking feeling in the pit of his stomach that they are coming to an end. Unlike the last days of term, which 'like a wounded snake drags its slow length along', the final days of the holidays flash past at an alarming speed. Suddenly there are a thousand things to be done, like climbing to the very top of the big oak tree, making a final attempt to catch the big trout which lies under the bridge, making it up with the gamekeeper's son for blacking his eye, and starting to do the homework which has to be handed in on the first day of term.

One task in particular which makes the final days of the holidays tolerable is the careful planning of what to take in one's tuck box. Because the food at most public schools is barely above the subsistence level, the contents of the tuck box have to be given much the same amount of thought as a yachtsman provisioning his ship for a round the world voyage.

Preparing a tuck box is a fine exercise in logistics. Is, for example, the space taken up by a large tin of assorted biscuits justified, or would it be better to settle for a couple of packets of Jaffa cakes and some extra tins of sliced peaches and mandarin oranges? How many tins of sardines and how many of Nestlés condensed milk? Strawberry jam or lemon curd? The problems are endless, not the least being what to include that you *don't* like to barter with another boy whose tuck box contains something you envy.

Mothers are very indulgent in the matter of filling tuck boxes, and only insist that you take an ample supply of writing paper for your weekly letter home. My recollection is that the only time one ever got a letter back was to complain if the weekly letter had not arrived.

7

The Alma Mater

THE existence of public schools seems to bother quite a few people. On one hand they deride them for being hotbeds of all manner of nameless vices, with sodomy and sadism as the main items in the curriculum. On the other hand the same critics lobby vigorously for their abolition on the grounds that they give their victims an unfair start in life.

Saki put the matter neatly when he wrote: 'You cannot expect a boy to be depraved until he has been to a good school.'

Less tongue-in-cheek, Henry Fielding declared public schools to be 'the nurseries of all vice and immorality.'

The confused picture is understandable amongst those who have attended less controversial educational establishments, because the confusion is caused largely by ex-public schoolboys themselves.

The trouble largely lies with the increasing number of rotters whose very rich parents have managed to squeeze them into a decent school and who then use it as a social crutch ever after. The Gentleman's Child, who regards attendance at his father's, grandfather's, and possibly great-grandfather's school as part of the penalty he has to pay for the accident of his birth, curls up with embarrassment when faced with the sort of conversational gambits which make critics of the system do the same.

The criterion of elitism in public schools is not so much how expensive they are, as how deeply steeped they are in tradition.

Westminster, for example, which dates from the early Middles Ages, is considered to be very much a public school, although a large proportion of the pupils are day boys.

The roll of ex-Westminster boys includes such illustrious names as Ben Jonson, Warren Hastings, and Christopher Wren. In more modern times, possibly the best-known Westminster old boy (who had the luck to arrive shortly after electricity was installed in 1923) is Kim ('third man') Philby, at the moment holding down a job as a Colonel in the KGB in Moscow.

Bores

Typical four-ale bar pronouncements by school bounder: 'A good thrashing never did anyone any harm. By God, when I was at school I got beaten every day of my life. Makes a man of you. Bring back hanging for the lower classes I say.'

Sociologists might ponder why none of this category of bore every says: 'A good thrashing never did anyone any harm. By God, when I was at school I used to thrash ten boys every day of my life. Made men of them. Bring back the lash I say.'

Is it perhaps considered less upper class to profess sadism rather than masochism?

Another of the Great Bores who give public schools a bad name is the name dropper. It only requires one of his

Managed to squeeze them into a decent school

contemporaries to attain modest public prominence for him to acquaint everyone within earshot of the fact:

'Did you see that Smithers has got a job in the new Cabinet shuffle? At school with him you know. As a matter of fact he was my fag. Lazy little blighter as I remember.'

If the number of people who claim to have had someone like Geoffrey Howe as their fag are telling the truth, it is surprising that our present Chancellor of the Exchequer ever had time to learn simple arithmetic.

And why is it that none of them ever seem to have been anyone else's fag?

Old school snobs

George Mackay Brown, in his excellent book about public schools, remarks that there are in fact only nine which can rightfully claim the distinction. If this is so, the dyed-in-the-wool school snob can readily get round the problem by reeling off the names of eight schools with undoubted claims to be included and adding his own, however undistinguished, as the ninth.

Indeed, it is those who went to the less traditional schools who are apt to rabbit on about it most. I can remember one particular offender in this category who, on being questioned more closely, turned out to have been at Gordonstoun.

School traditions

Before a new boy at the more traditional establishments even opens a text book he will discover that the first things he is required to learn are the traditions of his particular seat of learning.

These vary from place to place. At my own school the highest priority was given to learning the names of every corner of the buildings themselves and the surrounding grounds. Everything at school is called by some name whose origins are lost in the sands of time. Some were easy, like Big Cricket for the First Eleven pitch, but why Snipe Corner for an otherwise undistinguished corner of the playing fields, or 'the lantern' for an ugly little spire on the roof of Great Hall? Why was the headmaster known as the Grue (unless it was short for gruesome perhaps?) or prefects called 'beaks'?

Failure to answer a questionnaire on these subjects within twenty-four hours of arrival resulted in condign punishment.

Other certain ways of courting disaster were to fail to observe the proper etiquette. First year boys had to keep all three buttons of their jackets done up, second year boys could leave one undone, third year boys two, and in the fourth year they could swagger about displaying their prison-grey shirts in all their glory. It was a cardinal sin to run past a 'beak'. On sighting one of these grandees it was required to reduce speed to a sedate walk. Only sixth formers could walk on the quad grass, and so on, and so on.

I describe not men, but manners

If all this may seem bizarre to those whose schooldays have not been similarly complicated, it should be explained that it does not seem at all odd to the Gentleman's Child, simply because it is only an extension of his home life.

To give a simple example, a Gentleman will always address his butler, gardener, head keeper, and other members of his staff with whom he is on terms of close friendship by their surnames, as in, for example, to his gardener: 'Adams, why the hell is the asparagus so late?' By the same token, if any of his children were to call Adams anything but a respectful 'Mister Adams' they would be told off roundly for behaving above their station. Equally, the cook, whatever her marital status, is always accorded the dignity of Mrs, not only by the child but by the Gentleman and his wife.

It is all part of there being a right and a wrong way of doing things.

Schoolmasters

Whilst I have touched briefly on the subject of nicknames for one's fellow schoolboys, the nicknames for masters are a far more profound matter. It would indeed be true to say that the master who fails to receive the accolade of a nickname must regard himself in the same category as a civil servant who has been consistently passed over in the Queen's Birthday Honours list.

Some nicknames are predictable and unoriginal. A Mr Humphrey would almost inevitably be called Humpf, a master with a high-pitched voice Nancy, or one with a beard (unusual except for the very old) Moses. Other nicknames derive from idiosyncracies, such as Slogger, on account of his once being bowled first ball in the Master's match, or Hot-Lips on account of his being detected giving the matron a chaste kiss behind the squash courts.

Most schoolmasters are to a varying degree eccentric, and this becomes more marked as they become older. Not the least eccentric are those who have themselves been pupils at the school, who leave for only long enough to get a decent degree, and then return, like Mr Chips, to devote the rest of their lives to the service of their *alma mater*. There is a saying that old soldiers never die; they only fade away. This is much more true of schoolmasters, and old school-fellows meeting half a century after leaving can be heard to say incredulously, 'Do you know that old Bunny is *still* teaching the Lower Fourth First Steps in Latin?'

It must be said, however, that the eccentricities of masters at good schools do not extend to wearing safety pins in their ears or rings through their noses, which seem to be so much in vogue at other places.

Corporal Punishment

Because there is so much howdyedo about caning at schools, I make no apology for going into the matter more fully than I have already done, if only to point out the difference between the Gentleman's Child and those who do not have the same background.

It should be pointed out that the Gentleman seldom, if ever, chastises his own children. He has quite enough to do disciplining his own shooting dogs, or lashing his hunter over the last fence at a point-to-point, without having to bother with such trivialities. On the other hand, he is not the sort of chap who would go rushing to the Council for Civil Liberties if his boy is given four sharp cuts across the bum for picking his nose in class.

So far as the boy is concerned, to be caned is not regarded in at all the same light as it is by those whose parents are not paying through the nose for him to have the privilege. The comprehensive schoolmaster who retaliates for being given a vicious hack on the shins by putting the offender across his knee runs a severe risk of being punched on the nose by the little beast's father, reported to the headmaster, and probably sacked.

At the average public school, not only can an offender be caned by a master, but also by those among his schoolfellows who have risen to the eminence of prefects. On the whole, to be caned by a master not only holds greater prestige but is much more likely to be less painful. This is because some masters are so old and decrepit that they are scarcely able to raise a decent weal, whilst others are so myopic that half their strokes miss the mark altogether, and skid harmlessly up the victim's back. To be beaten by the Captain of Games is a very different matter indeed.

Whoever administers the punishment, however, the result is a matter of the greatest interest to fellow members of the victim's dormitory. They view the effect of a caning with the same critical interest as displayed by art critics on the first day of the Summer Exhibition at the Royal Academy. Wildly delivered strokes are greeted with hoots of derision, whilst six strokes delivered with such precision as to be inseparable (*extremely* painful) are greeted with undisguised admiration if not actual applause.

As for the victim, far from feeling degraded, he enjoys the admiration of his fellows in much the same way as if he had scored a try for the First Fifteen.

Bullying

Some boys are born bullies and some are born to be bullied. Every school of any category has its quota of Flashmans and Tom Browns, and the only compensation for the bullied at the more expensive schools is that his tormentor will certainly have a rich father, and possibly even a titled one. I agree, however, that this is something which can give little or no comfort unless the bullied is a crashing little snob.

To be beaten by the Captain of Games was a very
different matter indeed

Running away

If a boy finds himself being unmercifully bullied, beaten, or otherwise misused, he *must run away*. Like Sydney Carton, he will be doing a far, far better thing than he has ever done.

He will, of course, be recaptured fairly quickly and returned, but he will find that he will, from that moment on, enjoy a completely different status. He will be a hero, looked up to and admired by his schoolmates and even, though they would not admit it, by most of the masters.

When your recent chief tormentor comes up to you after second bell and says: 'I say, young Andrews, let me take you to the tuck shop and buy you a Mars Bar' it is heady stuff indeed. Like others, however, rocketed to overnight stardom, the fugitive should take it all with suitable modesty, or he may find that the euphoria does not last all that long.

Religion

Whether they like it or not, religion plays a large part in a young Gentleman's education. At the more traditional schools it is not unusual to have morning and evening chapel every day of the week, with a particularly heavy dose on Sundays.

The Sunday service in particular is made bearable by the sort of in-jokes that are unintelligible to the outsider, but a matter of the utmost hilarity to all schoolboys.

A good example of this sort of thing was the year when Prince Charles was made Head Boy (called 'the Guardian' for some odd reason) at Gordonstoun.

It so happened that that much-loved and respected prelate of the Church, the late Bishop of Moray, was to

fulfil one of his regular engagements to give the sermon
on the Sunday following Prince Charles's appointment.
The excellent Bishop had an unfortunate habit of using
the word 'really' with great frequency, so much so that
certain irreverent pupils were in the habit of taking
wagers on the number of times the word would be used.
They kept count by turning over a page of the hymnal on
each occasion.

Prince Charles finished his traditional inaugural
speech by saying:

'You will all know that our friend the Bishop of Moray
will be preaching here next Sunday. I am, of course,
quite well aware of a certain deplorable practice which
has become tradition on this solemn occasion. I must ask
you to discontinue this practice, as the rustling of the
pages of the hymnal every couple of minutes has grown to
such proportions as to make most of what I know will be a
very excellent sermon almost completely inaudible.'

There were few boys who could keep a straight face
when Sunday came around.

A more common occurrence which has the invariable
effect of reducing the whole school to fits of scarcely-
repressed giggles is when some dreadful boy chooses a
quiet moment of prayer to let off a resounding fart. It is
one of the golden rules of loyalty among schoolboys that
no-one must ever name the offender.

It is, however, only fair to add that few boys leave
school as confirmed atheists.

Games and lessons

To this end I neglected my lessons wherever possible
in that order. So much so that it is not much use being
good at lessons if you are not good at games.

Organised games are the very cornerstone of the competitiveness which the whole system is designed to achieve. It is gratifying for masters if you come high in the class lists, and may even earn you a rare grudging word of praise, but too much braininess can earn the reputation of being a swot by the less well mentally equipped, and this is not a passport to popularity.

I think I may mention here with becoming modesty that I myself was really rather brainy. However hard I tried to avoid being categorised as a swot I had the sort of infuriating brain which retained information however useless. Even to this day I have no difficulty in recalling that the Battle of Hastings took place in 1066 and that William Shakespeare not only wrote *Macbeth* but *The Merchant of Venice* as well.

On the other hand I had a great instinct for self-preservation, and quickly realised that if I could not at the very least make my house cricket eleven I would not come very high in the popularity stakes with my fellows.

To this end I neglected my lessons where ever possible and spent hours practising in the nets or working at the slip catch.

My industrious application had its reward. It was the practice to post the names of those picked for the school teams for forthcoming matches on the communal notice-board. I can remember the moment to this day.

Sauntering with deliberate slowness along the Cloister I glanced with feigned indifference at the notice board — and there it was! My name! 'The following have been selected, etc . . .' Half way down was D.C.H. Sutherland. I was so overcome with emotion that had not the obnoxious R.G. Miller been standing next to me I do believe I would have committed the unforgivable sin of blubbing.

Then, mercifully, the bell rang for tea, and as I climbed the stone steps to Great Hall an extraordinary thing happened. I suddenly realised that I had achieved everything I could possibly want from life. Here was I at the age of fifteen years and five months with my whole life stretching interminably before me, and I had nothing in the whole world left to strive for. By the time I reached the top of the stairs I was enveloped in a cloud of impenetrable gloom.

I am not sure that I have got over it yet.

8

Girls' Schools

IT WILL no doubt have been noticed that in this study of
the English Gentleman's Child I have appeared to assume
that Gentlemen's Children are exclusively boys.

This is not so. Many Gentlemen sire girls.

My excuse for this must be that from their nursery
days, until they are packed off to a boarding school, the
sexes are almost unidentifiable one from another.
Indeed, many little girls are more boyish than their
brothers, remonstrating strongly if they are required for
some special occasion to discard their tattered jeans or
corduroy trousers and be forced into a 'party frock', and
resolutely refusing to comb their hair so they come to look
more and more like Shetland ponies as they start to grow
up.

There are many male graduates from unisex nurseries
who would not agree with the nannie-ism: 'You must be
kind to your sister. Little girls are not as strong as little
boys.' This is the sort of dictum of which female
chauvinist pigs (sows?) are made. If her brother is
gentlemanly enough to desist from punching her in the
ribs, she will reward his chivalry by giving him a sharp
back-hander when Nannie isn't looking. It is of course a

well-known fact of life that little girls are given to pinching and pulling hair, which are generally not regarded as within the Queensberry Rules by little boys.

Playthings

By the same token, it should by no means be assumed that little girls prefer to play with dolls (particularly those dreadfully expensive ones that are advertised as: 'Realistic — Wet their own nappies'). In fact, they are perfectly happy with things like catapults and knives, or with a gadget for taking stones out of horses' hooves. This may be partly because Mummie and Daddie, with no hang-ups about keeping up with the Joneses, scarcely ever buy their children any toys at all, expecting them to make do with those which have survived their own childhood. It should be noted here that English Gentlemen, if they are sensible enough to hold on to their electric train sets, will gain more pleasure in the company of their daughters playing with this than they will with their sons. English Ladies like all trains, particularly those that take them to London to see their milliner, or an old school friend for lunch, or for various other tasks that can only be carried out in the capital.

Schooldays

Girls' boarding schools tend to be run on much the same line as boys'. There is the same emphasis on being good at games, the same importance placed on winning, and the same insistence on a rigid discipline.

Discipline

Although girls are not generally subjected to corporal punishment, the disciplinary methods used are infinitely

Looking more and more like Shetland ponies as they
start to grow up

more sadistic. After all, a summary whacking is over in a matter of minutes and, as we have seen, the victim might almost feel it worthwhile because of the admiration he earns from his contemporaries.

A common method of punishment in girls' schools for an offender is to be 'sent to Coventry'. This forces even her closest friends to demonstrate their hostility, even if they do not feel it. The fact that grown men resort to this particularly nasty 'girlish' device in trade union disputes does not make it any less reprehensible.

Indeed, whereas in boys' schools punishment is largely a highly personalised affair, the tendency in girls' schools is to attempt to hold the offender up to public ridicule and contempt. A girl, being caught out in, for example, telling a fib, would probably occasion the summonsing of the whole school to hear her confess to the awful crime.

One young lady at a very elevated establishment, who was caught picking a few gooseberries in the head-mistress's garden, was forced to wear a placard round her neck bearing the inscription: 'I am a thief. I was caught picking the headmistress's gooseberries.' She was not even allowed to remove the notice for Church, presumably so that there could not be any possibility that, by some mischance, God had not been informed of her heinous deed.

Games

In boys' schools, each term's new intake is judged largely by such physical characteristics as broad shoulders (indicating their future potential in the scrum). Similarly new girls are not looked upon as likely material to bring honour to the school by becoming possible winners of the Miss World competition, but rather by whether they have the jolly good thick legs so essential to success in the hockey field, or possibly possess a pair of expensive tennis racquets, which implies that they have a good deal of prowess in that particular field.

If anything, organised games at girls' schools are rather more robust than at boys' schools. Few games can offer more opportunity for violence than that most upper-class of all girls' games, Lacrosse. Not only does Lacrosse have practically no rules, but a Lacrosse pitch does not even have any boundaries, which allows personal vendettas to be fought out far from the actual scene of action.

Cricket, too, is a very popular game at girls' schools, representing as it is supposed to do the quintessence of all that is in the best British sporting tradition. Girls, by and large, are jolly good at cricket, and I suspect that it is only an oversight on the part of those responsible for administering the Sex Discrimination Act that we have not yet had a female Captain of the English Test team.

The sexual urge

By and large young ladies, because of the cloistered nature of their upbringing, are late developers in matters of sex. Of course, they would not be female if they did not have the usual passionate crushes on older girls, and there must be few who have not felt the first stirrings of desire at the sight of the games mistress tearing down the wing, displaying tantalising glimpses of white flesh and black suspenders under her short hockey tunic.

Their interest in boys, however, takes very much longer to develop. Not for them the indulgences of their sisters-under-the-skin who are scarcely into their 'teens before they start going through agonies of anticipation as St Valentine's day approaches, adorning every scrap of paper in sight with bleeding hearts pierced with arrows, and practising signing themselves Mrs John Travolta.

Young ladies, particularly those with brothers, regard the opposite sex with a deep-rooted suspicion, if not overt dislike. It is only when they are around fifteen, when their brothers start bringing their school-fellows home to stay for the hols that they begin to see the male of the species in a new light.

After that, of course, as everyone knows, there is no holding them.

Socially conscious

All of this is not to say that young ladies are not socially conscious in other matters. Forced during term-time to wear a uniform which permits no adornment, they die with embarrassment if their mothers turn up for Speech Day wearing an unsuitable hat, or talk in a loud voice all through Prize Giving. They can also be beastly little snobs, talking, for example, about Daddie's 'second gardener', so that everyone knows he has more than one. This is known as 'putting on dog' and frowned on by those who for one reason or another feel more socially secure.

The end product

When the young lady finally comes to leave her boarding school, if she has derived any benefit at all, she will have adequate control of her pony, a strong backhand at tennis, and a collection of cups, rosettes, and endless photographs of groups which will still have the power to bring a tear to her eye long after she has become a grand-mother.

The games mistress tearing down the wing

9

University

UNIVERSITIES for Gentlemen's Children are usually regarded as an optional extra. Of course, for those who from birth have been destined to go into one of the Services the question does not arise, nor for those whose future lies in running the family estates, nor for those who happen to be so thick that no university would touch them with a barge pole.

On the other hand, a spell at a university can do both the Gentleman's boys and girls a world of good. This has nothing to do with the possibility of great academic achievement, fitting them for High Office in the Civil Service in later life, but simply that the university provides a salutary antidote to all that has been inculcated at school.

It has already been remarked that the object of 'the system' is to imbue the Gentleman's Child with an ambition to succeed, and success is to play for the first fifteen, win the cross-country run, gain promotion from the ranks of the Officers' Training Corps, and even break through the intellectual stratosphere by becoming a member of the Upper Sixth.

Any boy who has achieved any or all of these ambitions may consider himself to have had a successful life, and nothing further should be expected of him. Certainly there are few who leave school imbued with a determination to be an astronaut, a captain of industry, or even an engine driver.

A few years reading history, or some equally relaxing subject, at a good university can do a great deal to change this deplorable lethargy. For the first time, he or she will meet other undergraduates with all manner of unimaginable ambitions (like becoming marine biologists or gaining first-class honours in Chinese) and all manner of new vistas will open.

Admittedly, the more seriously they take their gentlemanliness, the harder they will resist infection by the lower classes (for even Oxbridge is now virtually classless). They even go to the extent of forming those dreadfully incestuous clubs like the Pitt and the Bullingdon, where the members seem to spend all their time discussing who should be kept out, or donning fancy-dress clothes to try to demonstrate something or other. But there are other undergraduates, less ostentatious and, perhaps, more mature, who will try to attend as many lectures as they can with a view to scraping through a decent third class degree.

This is thoroughly laudable, but of course it should not be allowed to interfere with the desirability of obtaining a blue at some sport, which is far more likely to stand the Gentleman's Child in good stead in later life.

University habits

Critics of the university system are often heard to opine that the most likely things undergraduates learn are what

The most likely things undergraduates learn are their
sexual inclinations

their sexual inclinations are, and how best to cure a hangover. This is patently unfair. After leaving any school of any sort, the first thing all ex-pupils learn are their sexual inclinations and how best to cure a hangover. The only difference is that those who attend non-fee-paying schools are apt to learn the facts of life rather earlier than most.

One of the main things an undergraduate learns at university is that he or she is entitled to start a career halfway up the ladder.

One of the first things that a post-graduate learns is that this is not necessarily so.

Intellectuals

There are, of course, a large number of undergraduates of all social classes who take their chosen careers extremely seriously — notably future ministers of religion and possibly medical students when they are not researching the rival merits of Guinness or Newcastle Brown.

Intellectuals, on the other hand, are a race apart. Basically, they are sycophantic to a degree, sucking up to the more erudite dons and keeping meticulous diaries of their activities with which they intend to bore future generations when they come to write their memoirs.

In this they usually succeed. Few can resist an opening sentence like 'I so well remember that long summer at Oxford . . .' closely followed by an anecdote about Auden, or Isherwood, or Sitwell, or Waugh. The Bloomsbury Set were the worst at this but, perhaps fortunately, most of them have by now laid down their pens for the last time. Was Oxford a more intellectual ants' nest? Or was a Cambridge blue more prestigious?

I don't know. It's only that so few memoirs start 'I so well remember that long summer at Cambridge . . .'

closely followed by an anecdote about Burgess, Maclean, or Philby.

Just the same, there have been a lot of jolly decent chaps who first found their feet at some university. Those who did are a credit to 'the system' which has nursed them from the cradle to the Cabinet.

10

The Final Product

HAVING successfully completed the extraordinary battle course, which is perhaps the most accurate way of describing the upbringing of the Gentleman's Children, it is not surprising that they should tend to conform to a readily recognisable type.

Let it be said that this is not something they purposefully adopt in order to 'show up' others, but simply that 'the system' has been deliberately designed to produce a certain type, and it has to be an exceptional product of 'the system' on whom the marks do not show. In fact they are quite unaware of the tell-tale signs, and genuinely amazed when these are pointed out to them.

Gentlemanly expressions

Some ways in which gentlemen express themselves go right back to their nursery days. For example, no child would ever think of leaving the table after finishing his meal without first asking permission. As this politeness will have been impressed on him at an age when the chair legs were longer than his own, his request would be phrased as 'Nannie, may I get down please?'

Thus it is quite understandable that an elderly

Gentleman, bored by the interminable speeches at an official dinner, should turn to his neighbour and mutter: 'This chap's going on for ever. When the devil do you think they'll let us get down?' Only a foreigner, or someone who has not been brought up under nursery rules, would think the remark at all odd.

Foreigners

Gentlemen, by and large, make every allowance for foreigners who have an imperfect command of the English language. In this they show far greater sensitivity than the majority of people, who go to the other extreme by feeling so embarrassed at meeting foreigners that they actually resort to signs or baby language as a means of communication.

An example of this was the time when that worthy Labour Cabinet Minister, the late Jimmy Thomas, found himself seated at an official dinner next to the Chinese Ambassador, Mr Wellington Koo, surely one of the most charming emissaries to the Court of St James.

When the nauseating traditional turtle soup was served, Jimmy Thomas turned to Wellington Koo and enquired: 'Likee soupee?' Having received a polite acknowledgement he felt that he had discharged his conversational responsibilities and relapsed into silence for the rest of the meal.

Mr Koo, who, if I remember correctly, had been educated at Eton and Balliol, was later called upon to make a speech, and did so in the most impeccable unaccented voice. As he sat down to well-earned applause, he turned to Thomas and enquired smilingly: 'Likee speechee?'

In a similar situation a Gentleman would not have showed such sensitivity. Even if his neighbour could only speak an obscure Urdu dialect he would have subjected

Baby language as a means of communication

him to a discussion of the salmon fishing prospects throughout all of the eight courses.

Perhaps that is why Gentlemen are generally considered to make good Foreign Secretaries.

Food for thought

There is no occasion when a Gentleman's upbringing is so apparent as at meal times which, if the number of little books on etiquette are anything to go by, is the time when others feel least secure.

First of all there is the matter of vocabulary. There seems to be an increasing tendency amongst food writers and others to refer to the first course of any meal as 'starters', as if they were discussing the runners in the two-thirty at Ascot. An equally odd expression is 'afters'. The average Gentleman asked when dining out in a restaurant what he would like for 'afters' would in all probability reply; 'a fast taxi and a quick romp in the hay'. What, he wonders, perhaps with some justification, is wrong with 'the first course' and 'the pudding'?

Another word that grates on the ear is 'trimmings' as in: 'Then we had the most lovely turkey with all the trimmings'. What on earth does it mean?—but there we go again rattling on about all those U and non-U words which, to my mind, is a very non-U thing to do indeed. We will be complaining about calling a sitting room a 'lounge' next. Gentlemen, of course, do not lounge.

Good manners

It is generally conceded that all Gentlemen, however beastly in other ways, have good manners, and it is as good a definition of a Gentleman as any to say that he is someone who is never *unintentionally* rude. When he wants to be he is capable, of course, of being very rude indeed.

Good manners at table come as naturally to the Gentleman who has been through 'the system' as washing behind the ears.

I remember my first salutary lesson when lunching with the rather irascible father of a schoolfellow. When I rather timidly asked him if I might have another potato, he handed me the dish from which I was about to help myself, and let the whole thing crash onto the table (whilst his wife raised her eyes and uttered a silent imprecation). Never again did I commit the solecism of not first taking the dish from the person who offered it before helping myself.

My own father had an equally salutary way of impressing good manners on his guests. Anyone dining with him who was not aware that it was extremely rude, when declining a further glass of wine, to signify this by placing his or her hand over the top of the glass was in for an awakening when the butler, on my father's orders, continued to pour the wine over the offender's hand until it was removed.

The generally accepted practice is, of course, to allow your glass to be filled, and if you do not want any more, not to drink any more. This is a practice of which butlers thoroughly approve, as one of their traditional perquisites is the wine left over in visitors' glasses.

Wine snobbery

If there is one form of snobbery of which a properly brought up young Gentleman can never be accused it is over the question of wine.

I can remember once lunching with one of our more pompous wine writers who actually ordered the waiter to remove the *coq au vin* on the grounds that the wine used in cooking it was non-vintage. There can be few who have not curled up with embarrassment when their host in a restaurant, determined to demonstrate that he 'knows what's what', sends back a perfectly sound bottle of wine on the grounds that it is not to his taste. In cases like this a good wine waiter will simply return with an identical bottle to be greeted with a beam of approval from the boor who feels he has made his point.

Most Gentlemen's Children are permitted to drink wine, albeit sometimes watered, from a comparatively early age. Thus they early on acquire a preference for red or white, claret or Burgundy, or anything else, and will drink their preference with any food despite the horrified glances of those who believe it to be sacrilege (let alone non-U) to drink a decent claret with fish.

Equally, no Gentleman would serve champagne in those little shallow glasses like inverted brassieres for dwarf ladies, cover the label of a wine being served with a napkin, or circulate the after-dinner port from left to right.

I make these points only to defend young Gentlemen if they sometimes appear at worst odd or at best pedantic. Don't blame them. Blame 'the system'.

Deportment for Ladies

Of course, all Ladies of whatever station in life are early made aware of the dangers of occupying a lavatory seat before the chain has stopped swinging, but most young Ladies of quality will also go into adult life warned of the impropriety of occupying an armchair so recently vacated by a Gentleman that the cushions are still warm.

They will also have in-built Nannie-isms such as always sitting upright (especially in railway carriages), 'lounging' of course being one of the most carnal sins of deportment. The right sort of girls' schools even have badges for good deportment, and it is a matter of great shame to have this

Continued to pour the wine

removed because of being seen *lolling* in the dining room.

Ladies may also have certain *idées fixes* derived from well-meaning, usually frustrated, female relations. For example, my own daughter, staying over a wet half-term with a maiden aunt, asked her somewhat querulously why it always seemed to rain at the weekends, to which Auntie replied in a low, conspiratorial voice: 'Well, you see dear, God does not really like the working classes'.

My daughter, to give her her due, considered this most unjust of God and held it against Him for many years.

Other characteristics

Of course there are many other ways in which young gentlemen newly launched into an uncaring world manage either to give offence to the more touchy or become figures of fun to the more tolerant.

There is no doubt that they are at their most intolerable when two or more are gathered together.

Then they tend to talk in loud voices and, particularly if they went to the same school, discuss matters of which any outsider unfortunate enough to find himself in their company can have no possible knowledge of or interest in.

Attitudes to money

Most young ladies and gentlemen are 'careful' with money. This is largely because the amount they are permitted to take to school with them to cover such extras as toothpaste or fizzy drinks and sweets at the tuck shop is extremely limited, and it is only by the exercise of the utmost restraint that it can be made to last the whole term.

Thus, just as it would be an act of reckless folly to stand one's friend a stick of sherbet in the tuck shop, so in later life, in many Gentlemen's clubs, it is not done to stand a fellow member a whisky and soda. Equally, as credit was

Any outsider unfortunate enough to find himself in
their company

strictly forbidden at tuck shops, Gentlemen on the whole do not carry credit cards, but limit themselves to credit accounts with their tailor and wine merchant.

When later, either through inheritance or paternal benevolence, they have access to enough money to warrant opening a bank account, it is only the minority who lose their heads completely and drive the unfortunate bank manager to an early grave.

When they marry they *never* have joint accounts with their wives. In fact most of them think it a jolly silly thing to marry a wife who does not have a healthy account of her own.

Ostentation

A Gentleman's Children are brought up to deride anything that might be considered ostentatious. Just as the young male does not adorn himself with rich geegaws, so the young female does not overdress. Oddly enough, this characteristic is often more marked in young ladies who nowadays wear such outrageously eccentric garments as to defeat their own purpose. There are those among the older generation who consider the bra-less, tattered jeans, barefoot look ostentatious.

Tipping

As further demonstration of the complex life-style which comes naturally to the Gentleman's Child, it is only necessary to have a look at the 'rules' governing tipping.

Always tip your soup plate away from you when finishing ('Nannie does not want to see the bottom of Henry's soup plate, does she?'.)

Always tip your pudding plate towards you. (Why Nannie should not mind seeing the bottom of Henry's pudding plate is a mystery which is never questioned.)

Never tip your chair backwards. (Practical. It is probably Chippendale and fragile.)

Never tip your hat to a lady. (Always *raise* your hat and count three before replacing it.)

Never tip waiters or others too heavily. (It is ostentatious as well as being economically unsound.)

Aides memoirs

From their very earliest days Gentlemen's Children are either intimidated or cajoled into proper behaviour by proscribed reading, largely in verse. The foremost work of intimidation is *Shockheaded Peter*, which describes in vivid detail the awful fate which awaits such miscreants as Fidgety Phil who Could Not Sit Still, and the girl who could not resist playing with matches.

Amongst the chief cajolers are the verses of Robert Louis Stevenson:

> A child should always say what's true,
> And speak when he is spoken to,
> And behave mannerly at table:
> At least as far as he is able

and:

> Children, you are very little,
> And your bones are very brittle;
> If you would grow up great and stately,
> You must try to walk sedately.

There must be few Gentlemen's Children who do not know such admonitory verses as:

Never, never let your gun
Pointed be at anyone.
All the pheasants ever bred
Won't repay for one man dead

or:

On the first of September one Sunday
  morn,
I shot a hen pheasant in standing corn,
Without a licence, contrive who can
A greater collection of crimes against
  God and man.

So there you have the Gentleman's Children. To many
they may seem to be complex personalities, but in reality
they are simple folk almost to the point of naivety.

If one had to sum up everything that 'the system' is
designed to teach them, it is to be found in one single
verse by Sir Henry Newbolt:

There's a breathless hush in the Close
  tonight—
Ten to make and the match to win—
A bumping pitch and a blinding light,
An hour to play and the last man in.
And it's not for the sake of a ribboned
  coat,
Or the selfish hopes of a season's fame.
But his Captain's hand on his shoulder
  smote—
'Play up! Play up! and play the game!'

Epilogue
Of course, 'the system' does not always work.

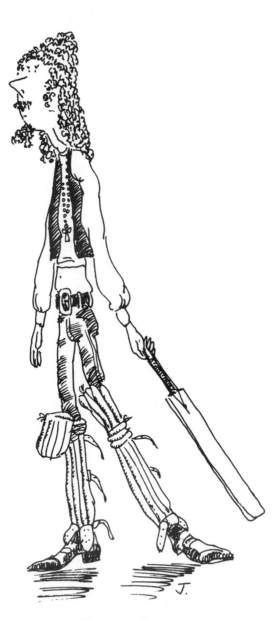

Play up, play up

Epilogue

Of course, 'the system' does not always work.